KU-676-584

Why
do people harm
Animals?

Chris Mason

179.3

ST. CUTHBERT'S HIGH SCHOOL
NEWCASTLE UPON TYNE NE15 7PN

HODDER
Wayland

an imprint of Hodder Children's Books

© 2001 White-Thomson Publishing Ltd

Produced for Hodder Wayland by
White-Thomson Publishing Ltd
2/3 St Andrew's Place
Lewes
BN7 1UP

Series concept: Alex Woolf
Editor: Philip de Ste. Croix
Cover design: Hodder Children's Books
Inside design: Stonecastle Graphics Ltd
Consultant: Sue Dawson of the RSPCA
Picture research: Shelley Noronha –
    Glass Onion Pictures
Indexer: Amanda O'Neill

Published in Great Britain in 2001 by Hodder
Wayland, an imprint of Hodder Children's Books
This paperback edition published in 2002
The right of Chris Mason to be identified as the
author has been asserted by him in accordance
with the Copyright, Designs and Patents Act 1988.

All rights reserved. No part of this publication may
be reproduced, stored in a retrieval system, or
transmitted, in any form or by any means without
the prior written permission of the publisher, nor
be otherwise circulated in any form of binding or
cover other than that in which it is published and
without a similar condition being imposed on the
subsequent purchaser.

British Library Cataloguing in Publication Data
Mason, Chris
 Why do people harm animals?
 1. Animal welfare 2. Animal welfare –
 Moral and ethical aspects
 I.Title
 179.3

ISBN 0 7502 37198

Printed and bound in Italy by
G. Canale & C.S.p.A. Turin

Hodder Children's Books
A division of Hodder Headline Limited
338 Euston Road, London NW1 3BH

Picture acknowledgements
The publisher would like to thank the following
for their kind permission to use their pictures:
AKG Berlin, 8; Associated Press, (cover) (Great Falls
Tribune), 35 (Michel Euler), 39 (Denis Poroy), 43
(Louise Buller); Camera Press, 4 (Brian Snyder), 16
(J. Kopec), 33 (bottom) (Darren Regnier); James
Davis Travel Photography, 18; Durrell Wildlife
Conservation Trust, 37; Ecoscene, (contents)
(bottom) (Michael Gore), 7, 26 (Sally Morgan), 34
(Michael Gore); Family Life Pictures, 19 (top)
(Angela Hampton); FLPA, 30 (Terry Whittaker);
Robert Harding Picture Library, 20 (bottom)
(R. Maisonneuve), 25 (Kodak), 36 (bottom), 40
(J. Lightfoot), 44 (Bildagentur Schuster); Hodder
Wayland Picture Library, 6 (bottom), 14, 19
(bottom), 20 (top), 21 (Dorian Shaw), 23 (bottom);
Impact, 22 (Bruce Stephens), 42 (Philippe Gontier);
Panos Pictures, (contents) (top), 17; Popperfoto,
(imprint page) (Paul Hackett, Reuters), 10 (John
Hrusa, Reuters), 11 (Corinne Dufka, Reuters), 12
(Greg Garay, Reuters), 13 (Andrew Winning), 15
(Jason Reed, Reuters), 24, 32 (Paul Hackett,
Reuters); RSPCA Photolibrary, 5, 6 (top), 9 (Philip
Meech), 28 (Nathan Strange), 31, 33 (top), 38
(Louise Murray/Wild Images); Science Photo
Library, 45 (Simon Fraser); Still Pictures, 27 (Dylan
Garcia), 29 (Matthew Wanner), 41 (Peter
Weimann); Topham Picturepoint, 23 (top).

Cover picture: A coyote caught in a leg trap near
Fort Benton in Montana, USA.

Contents

ST CUTHBERT'S HIGH SCHOOL
NEWCASTLE UPON TYNE NE15

1. How can people do that?

What is cruelty?

Every year the Canadian government allows the killing of more than 250,000 seals for their meat, fur and other body parts. Most of the seals, many of them cubs, are clubbed to death, their blood staining red the ice on which they die. Pictures of this hunt, or harvest as the sealers prefer to call it, have caused protests around the world. 'Stop this cruelty', say the campaigners. But it doesn't stop because not everybody agrees that the hunt is cruel or should be stopped. The Canadian government says that there are plenty of seals, that the hunt is properly controlled and that the hunters do their best to avoid inflicting unnecessary pain. Who is right?

'I think that the worst kind of cruelty is being unfair to animals when you're fed up with them and can't be bothered. If you have a pet, you have to realize how you've got to change when you get one.'
George Cooper, aged 12, who has a wire-haired fox terrier, Bob

◀ *A seal hunter raises a club to beat a seal unconscious during the annual Canadian seal hunt. Seals are killed in this way chiefly for their skins.*

Are you cruel? No. Have you ever been cruel? Well, maybe you have but it was a little thing and you didn't really mean it. Would you be cruel to animals? You probably wouldn't.

Most of you who read this book will answer these questions in a similar way. Of course we all sometimes say or do something that is cruel but being cruel is not easy. We soon learn that it causes pain and suffering and almost all of us regret doing that, especially to animals.

Unfortunately, some people are cruel to animals. Governments and charities around the world work hard to protect animals and yet hundreds of thousands of cases of cruelty to animals are reported every year. Why is this?

▲ *This pony was left to starve to death by his owners. Luckily an animal charity, the RSPCA, rescued him. This is how he looked after several weeks of care and attention.*

Why are people cruel to animals?

Cases of cruelty include people mistreating their pets, people neglecting their animals, farm animals being caused unnecessary suffering and deliberate acts of cruelty by those who want to inflict misery on animals for fun.

Some people don't mean to be cruel. They do not know or understand what they are doing. A lot of people unknowingly cause pain and suffering to their pets because they don't know how to look after them. Sheer ignorance is one of the main causes of cruelty to pets all over the world, but good advice will often help to overcome the problem.

▲ A solitary bear reaching out from its cage at a zoo in Borneo. Large animals like this seem unhappy living in such cramped conditions.

◀ A catch of fish from a trawler being sorted by the fishermen. We are used to seeing scenes like this, but many people argue that it is cruel to animals.

Others do not believe that what they are doing is cruel. Some, but not all, sports hunters and people who fish use practices that cause pain and suffering to wild animals. They do not see these as cruel, just necessary. They are often very defensive and upset when people accuse them of cruelty.

So why are people cruel to animals? Can we agree on what is cruel and what isn't? Can we stop people being cruel? To answer these questions we need to find out more by looking at the facts and listening to people who work with and care for animals. This book will help you to answer the questions for yourself.

▼ Pilot whales are hunted and killed for their meat by people living in the Faeroe Islands. To the islanders, this is a perfectly normal annual tradition.

case study · case study · case study · case study · case study

Every year the people of the Faeroe Islands in the north Atlantic carry out the *Grindadrap*, the hunting and killing of up to 1,500 pilot whales, which is a tradition going back hundreds of years. The whales are driven to the shore by powerboats and then killed with special long knives. Opponents of the hunt say that it is barbaric. Leivur Janus Hansen, a Faeroese, says, 'What do you think is more humane: to have an animal living in a cage all of its life, or to let it roam free from birth to death? Do you think that going to the clean disinfected supermarket for your meat is more natural than a bloody and messy hunt?'

2. Caring for animals

People and animals

People have always lived close to animals. Early humans hunted animals for food but they soon learned that it was sometimes easier to capture and breed animals to kill for food. We don't know when people first started keeping animals as pets or companions, but pictures from early times show what seem to be tame dogs and cats.

The ancient Egyptians kept and even worshipped cats. The goddess Bastet (sometimes called Pasht) had a cat's head. The Egyptians would often mourn the death of a cat and were said to have surrendered the city of Pelusium to the Persians to save hundreds of hostage cats that the Persian army had captured. Unfortunately people have not always been so kind to the animals they keep. The Egyptians even had punishments for those who harmed or killed cats.

Organizations such as the United States-based American Society for the Prevention of Cruelty to Animals (ASPCA) and the Royal Society for the Prevention of Cruelty to Animals (RSPCA) in Britain were set up during the nineteenth century.

▼ *An American coal miner photographed with a pit pony in the nineteenth century. The animals had to endure very harsh working conditions underground.*

The founders of these and many other animal welfare charities around the world were horrified by the treatment of domestic and farm animals, particularly horses which, before the widespread use of steam and petrol engines, provided the power for many forms of transport.

They set up teams of inspectors who could prosecute people for cruelty to animals. They also established clinics and shelters for sick and abandoned animals. Both organizations stress the importance of education and public information work in stopping cruelty. They provide materials to help teachers and children understand more about the humane treatment of animals.

An RSPCA inspector examining a pet rabbit. Animal welfare charities like the RSPCA help to educate people in how to treat animals responsibly.

FACT:
The Society for the Prevention of Cruelty to Animals (SPCA) was founded in 1824 in the UK. In that year it had 149 people convicted for cruelty. The Royal Society for the Prevention of Cruelty to Animals (RSPCA), as it is now known, investigated 132,000 suspected cruelty cases in England and Wales in 1999. The society found new homes for 100,000 animals.
RSPCA ONLINE http://www.rspca.org

Caring for animals

In 1917 Maria Dickin set up PDSA (the People's Dispensary for Sick Animals) in Whitechapel, then a very poor part of London's East End. She was shocked by the suffering of the animals belonging to poor people who could not afford to pay for veterinary treatment. She opened a small clinic offering free care to help deal with this problem.

▼ *Helpers release some of the African penguins that were cleaned up after an oil spill in June 2000 off Cape Town, South Africa. The birds were fouled by fuel leaking from a sunken oil tanker.*

PDSA now has 45 PetAid animal hospitals throughout Britain that treat around 1.3 million pets a year. The charity still offers free veterinary care to pet owners who cannot afford to pay for the necessary treatment.

case study · case study · case study · case study · case study

In June 2000 a massive oil spill off Cape Town, South Africa, threatened tens of thousands of African penguins on Robben and Dassen Islands. Amongst the volunteers who helped with rescuing and washing the affected birds were many students from local schools. Younger children like Rachel (8) and Shannon (11) Bernhardt, and their friend Kaya Kuhn (8), produced a newsletter, 'Penguin Post', and organized collections of money to help the rescue effort, and toothbrushes and towels for cleaning oil off the birds.

PDSA also recognizes the need for education and runs Pet Protectors, a club that teaches children from the age of five upwards about responsible pet ownership. Young people in their teens also support the organization's work through the PDSA Youth Challenge.

The International Fund for Animal Welfare (IFAW), a USA-based international campaigning organization, works using protest and publicity to stop cruelty. It has campaigned against the annual Canadian seal hunt, whaling, fox-hunting and the ivory trade.

IFAW concentrates on opposing the killing of wild animals such as whales and elephants for commercial profit, protecting the habitat of wild animals and, increasingly, rescuing animals in distress following natural or people-made disasters, such as oil spills.

> 'It's time to say enough and insist that our coastlines, their communities and the animals that live there are properly protected.'
> *Sarah Scarth, IFAW's Emergency Relief Co-ordinator, after a large oil spill off the South African coast*

▼ *A huge pile of confiscated ivory being burned by an officer of the Kenya Wildlife Service.*

Animals that help people

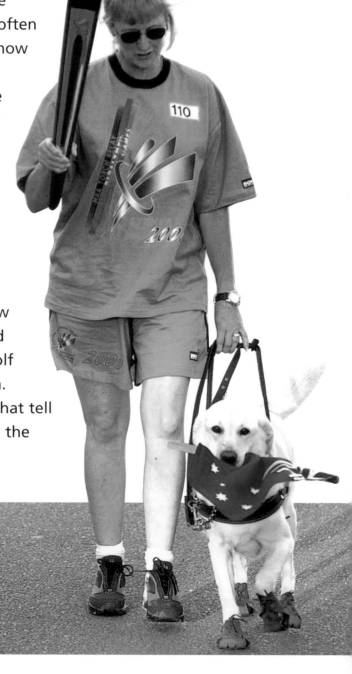

▼ Sue-Ellen Lovett with her seeing-eye dog during the Sydney 2000 Paralympic Torch relay in Australia.

Sometimes animals, either domesticated or wild, look after us. Seeing-eye dogs for the blind and those used in search and rescue missions are obvious examples. People who work with and keep horses will often talk of their special relationship and how the animal has helped them at important times. There are many true stories of dolphins rescuing or guiding to shore people in danger of drowning, or drifting in boats lost near land.

In different cultures throughout the world, tales of animals, often with magical powers, helping people are common. For example, stories tell how fish help west African villagers to find water during a drought, or an old wolf keeps a dying man company in Russia. Native Americans have many stories that tell of special bonds between people and the animals around them.

It seems that people today have lost some of the respect for animals that these ancient stories communicate.

Animals are now often used in therapy to help people with illnesses or disability. Health professionals have come to realize that contact with animals can aid recovery or development. In the USA there are over 2,500 programmes using animals in this way.

A horse called Pete is one of these therapeutic animals. He suffered neglect and cruelty before being brought to the Cape Cod Therapeutic Riding Center where he works with children with disabilities. He is particularly sensitive to the needs of children who have either Down's syndrome or cerebral palsy, compensating for their poor balance or lack of control. No-one at the centre doubts the benefits to the children of riding on Pete.

▲ *A two-year-old child with learning difficulties closes his eyes as a dolphin in an aquarium at a Mexico zoo nudges him gently. This is part of a type of therapy aimed at stimulating the child's brain.*

CUTHBERT'S HIGH SCHOOL
NEWCASTLE UPON TYNE NE15 7PX

3. Pets - companions or victims?

What do pets mean to us?

People in the United States are expected to spend $29 billion on their pets in the year 2001. This amount, which is more than the governments of some poorer countries spend in total, shows how important pets, or what some people call companion animals, are in countries like the USA and Britain.

No longer are pets just fed scraps. Pet owners can now buy 'gourmet' and 'diet' products for their pets and, if they are wealthy and perhaps a little unusual, they can even buy jewellery and small coats for their pet dogs or cats.

▼ *People around the world love their pets, but some owners do not think enough about the needs of the animals themselves before they buy them.*

Over 60 per cent of US households own pets. In Britain there are 7.5 million pet cats, 7 million pet dogs, 1 million pet rabbits and hundreds of thousands of smaller pet animals, such as fish and rodents. Most of these pets are well cared for and happy with their owners.

Sometimes, though, it seems that the way in which we show love for our pets does them more harm than good. A growing number of dogs and cats are treated by vets for weight problems; their owners are feeding them too much and exercising them too little.

Some of the animals that we keep as pets are really not suited to living with people. Rabbits do not like being handled and prefer fresh air to a hutch indoors. Goldfish are very sensitive to noise; a tap on their tank can terrify them. Hamsters like to live in holes and become so distressed when picked up that they can suffer heart attacks.

When we buy a pet, we often think more about our own enjoyment than considering the animal's welfare.

▲ *More and more money is spent on pampering pets every year – sometimes with the strangest results! This poodle is taking part in a dog-grooming show in Bangkok, Thailand.*

FACT:
A recent survey of pet owners in the USA found that:
28 per cent talk to pets on their telephones,
27 per cent celebrate their pets' birthdays with parties,
37 per cent carry pictures of their pets in their wallets.
PetsMart, 2000

Should we keep exotic pets?

Some people like to keep what are called exotic pets. These unusual animals, such as spiders, snakes, turtles and even monkeys and large wild cats, can be very difficult to look after. They often come from very different habitats from ours. They may need to be kept really warm and to be fed on food, sometimes other live animals, that comes from their natural homeland.

Many exotic pet owners look after their animals well but some find that they cannot cope. Reptiles in particular cause problems as they grow and they are often turned out into the wild where they soon become ill and die.

▼ *This owner keeps a very unusual mixture of pets; this group includes a dog, a warthog and a lioness.*

The trade in exotic pets is growing and some of it is illegal. Some animals from Asia, Latin America and Africa are rare, sometimes in danger of extinction, and they are often popular with collectors. People earn a lot of money by capturing and selling rare monkeys, reptiles, wild cats and birds to collectors in other countries.

International law forbids the trade in these endangered animals and governments and customs officials work hard to stop the trapping and smuggling of them. Despite their efforts, however, animals continue to be trapped and many of them die while being transported to other countries, packed into unsuitable boxes and crates where they suffocate or starve.

▲ *A variety of small mammals are crammed into cages at an animal market in Quanzhan, China.*

case study · case study · case study · case study · case study

In 1995 Philippines customs officers discovered two drills, rare rainforest monkeys from Africa, in a smuggled consignment of exotic pets bound for collectors in Asia. Animal welfare agencies, with the help of the Philippines government, the airline Lufthansa and the oil company Mobil, organized their return to a refuge in Nigeria 13,000 kilometres away.

Within a year the drills were ready for release back into the wild. To the surprise and pleasure of everyone involved, one of the drills gave birth just before her release.

4. On the farm

Feeding the world

There are more people on earth than ever before. Since 1960 the world population has doubled. It now stands at over 6 billion in 2001. Most of these people, particularly those who live in towns and cities, who amount to over half the world's population, rely on farmers to feed them.

People who live in richer countries such as Britain, Canada and the USA eat more meat, particularly 'fast food' like hamburgers and fried chicken, than ever before. This trend is spreading to other countries, such as India, where US-owned fast food companies are opening outlets. When people buy meat in supermarkets or meals at burger bars, they expect it to be cheap. If it is not, they go somewhere else. So lots of people want more and more cheap meat and farmers have to produce it.

FACT:
Every year over 100 million pigs are raised in the USA. Sometimes up to 10,000 pigs are kept in one huge building.
FactoryFarming.com; and The News & Observer, Raleigh, North Carolina, February 1995

▼ *Food stands like this cater to people who want their food fast and cheap.*

Most meat-eating Europeans and North Americans expect to be able to buy reasonably priced beef, lamb, chicken and pork, as well as milk from cows and eggs from chickens. The supermarkets that most people buy from are part of a huge and complex industry.

The farms that produce most of these animals are not like the picture that many of us have of a farm: a few small buildings and barns, some fields, a herd of 20–30 cows, a duck pond and chickens roaming in the farmyard. To meet the growing demand for cheap meat and to make a profit, farms have now become what are called factory farms: huge businesses with hundreds or thousands of penned animals being raised in factory units. The more animals there are in a 'unit', the more efficient the farm will be, and the more money it will make.

▲ *Many modern farms exist to produce meat for sale in butcher's shops.*

▼ *Not all farms look like this; many are run more like industrial factories.*

Factory or free-range?

Many people believe that factory or intensive farming – where animals are raised in ways that get the most meat, milk or eggs from them – is cruel. Cows, which have a natural lifespan of twenty to twenty-five years, may now produce 40 per cent more milk than twenty years ago, but they do not live for more than five years before 'burning out' and being sent to slaughter.

Hens kept in battery cage systems live four in a cage that has a floor the size of a piece of writing paper. They cannot flap their wings or exercise their legs. The windowless shed in which they live may hold up to 90,000 other birds. The European Union (EU) is now phasing out battery production and replacing it with intensive systems that allow the birds more space and some freedom.

▲ Chicks being raised in a battery-type poultry house are tipped out from boxes on to the floor of the unit.

◀ Intensive methods of farming mean that many routine operations on the farm, such as delivering feed to the animals, are now mechanized.

Because many people think that this kind of intensive rearing is cruel, a growing number of farmers are turning to free-range farming. In this system the animals have much more room when kept indoors, and are allowed to roam around more when they are outside.

Free-range chickens, for example, though kept on perches in barns, often in large numbers, are able to move freely both within the barn and outdoors, and they can behave as birds naturally do, dust-bathing, stretching and flapping their wings.

The RSPCA has established a set of guidelines for farmers and retailers, called the Freedom Food Scheme, which helps to encourage this cruelty-free approach to animal rearing.

▲ *Free-range ducks and chickens, such as these birds seen in a French farmyard, enjoy much better living conditions than poultry kept in battery cages.*

'We give our animals good home-grown food, plenty of fresh air, roomy and well-bedded winter quarters and as short a journey to market as possible because we want them to live as well as they can without stress or suffering.'
Ruth and Mike Downham, organic farmers in Cumbria, UK

Farming the seas

Many people see fish farming, or aquaculture, as a way of meeting our food needs without cruelty. Fish farming has been practised for centuries in Asia and parts of Africa. The new farms, though, are larger and more intensive, like land-based factory farms.

Instead of being caught in the wild, sea fish and shellfish, such as salmon and shrimp, and freshwater fish, like trout and tilapia, are raised in floating pens fixed to the river or sea bed. The fish are bred in hatcheries and then raised in larger pens where they are fed special food. When they are fully grown, the fish can be easily removed from the pens, killed and sent for sale.

Aquaculture now produces around a quarter of the world's fish supply. If you have eaten salmon, shrimp or trout recently, the chances are that it was raised on a fish farm.

FACT:
Fish farming is one of the fastest-growing agricultural industries in the world. One in five fish eaten by people is produced in a fish farm.
Food and Agriculture Organization of the United Nations

◀ *A salmon hatchery in the Highlands of Scotland – once the young fish have hatched, they are reared in pens until they are ready to be killed and eaten.*

Some people feel that fish farming can be cruel. Salmon are carnivores, which means that they eat other marine animals. When they are raised in captivity, they have to be fed food made from other fish and shellfish. It can take up to 5 kg of wild fish to raise 1 kg of farmed fish. Tilapia and some other freshwater fish do not need animal-based feed; they survive on a more sustainable plant-based diet.

The pens produce a lot of pollution from the uneaten food, fish waste and the chemicals used to treat the fish. This pollution can affect other more sensitive animals. The main worry is that the fish are crowded into the pens and enjoy none of the freedom of movement that a wild fish has. The crowding can be a particular problem at feeding time or when the fish are moved, and can lead to distress, injury and death.

▲ Wild salmon are naturally strong and vigorous fish; those bred in fish farms have to survive in cramped conditions.

◀ Not all the fish on the fishmonger's slab come from the open seas; up to 20 per cent of them are likely to have been reared on fish farms.

5. Animals on show

All the fun of the circus?

Many young people first see large animals, such as tigers, bears and elephants, in circuses. There's no doubt that many children are excited and happy to see, smell and hear animals that they have only previously seen on television or in films.

Many people, though, feel that making animals perform in circuses is wrong. Elephants in the wild do not stand upright on tubs, wild bears do not ride little bikes, tigers don't have to jump though flaming hoops. Circus animals have to be trained to do the tricks that people expect to see. Very often the training is cruel and unnatural. When not being trained, the animals are kept in cages, enclosures or travelling wagons that are quite different from their natural environment. The space for the animals is cramped and unpleasant.

▼ *This chimpanzee, dressed up as a soccer player, has been taught to perform tricks.*

To many people the worst thing about circuses is that they cause us to see wild animals in the wrong way. An elephant in a little dress loses its natural dignity. In the wild a female Asian elephant, the type most often used in circuses, may lead a family for decades, ranging over a wide territory and forming deep and caring relationships. Spending a life in chains and performing tricks in front of children is not natural behaviour for an elephant.

The supporters of circuses say that at least they allow people to see animals that they would not otherwise see close up. Their opponents say that rather than treating magnificent wild animals as performers in a show, it would be better not to see them at all.

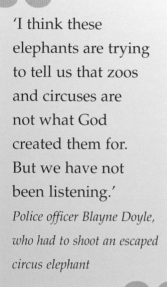

'I think these elephants are trying to tell us that zoos and circuses are not what God created them for. But we have not been listening.'

Police officer Blayne Doyle, who had to shoot an escaped circus elephant

◀ *Lots of people enjoy the thrill of seeing wild animals in a circus, but others think that making animals perform like this takes away their natural dignity.*

At the zoo

The earliest recorded zoo was that of the ancient Egyptian Queen Hatshepsut, who in the fifteenth century BC sent an expedition to the Red Sea to collect exotic animals. Like many of the zoos that were set up in the following centuries all around the world, Hatshepsut's zoo was created mainly for her entertainment and to show off her wealth and power.

The menagerie at the Tower of London, created by King John in the twelfth century, was opened to the public in the seventeenth century, the main attraction being animal baiting. In seventeenth-century France, on the other hand, King Louis XIV's zoo was open to scientists who studied and learned about the captive animals.

▼ *The giraffes in London Zoo are kept in large, open enclosures rather than being locked up behind bars in cages.*

London Zoo, which took over the Tower menagerie, was created in 1826. It followed the French example and soon became a centre for scientific study.

Modern zoos seek to balance entertainment for their customers with the needs and welfare of the animals. Instead of empty cages and ugly pens, the animals live in surroundings that resemble their natural habitats.

▼ Some people argue that wonderful animals, like this rhino, do not belong in a zoo in the centre of a city.

Sometimes zoos make such realistic habitats to keep their animals happy that visitors cannot always see them! Some zoos have stopped keeping certain animals, such as bears, because it is felt that it is too cruel to keep them penned in captivity.

Zoos also seek to save endangered species by breeding them in captivity and then releasing the animals back into the wild. Some people feel that despite all this good work, zoos are still prisons for animals and that it would be better if more money was spent on protecting them in the wild.

Performing sea creatures

A new trend in animal entertainment is the growth of centres and theme parks devoted to sea life. These twenty-first century aquaria attract the same type of criticism as zoos because they use captive animals, but they defend themselves by pointing out the high standard of care that they provide for their animals.

Sea Life Centres in Britain are very popular with schools and young people. The 'walk through' layout takes visitors past and even under glass tanks that allow them to see marine animals in a version of their natural habitat. The centres are primarily for entertainment but they also offer a great deal of information and education. The Sea Life Centres do not keep larger marine animals captive as they feel that this would be cruel.

▼ *A killer whale performing for the crowd at the Sea World marine park, San Diego, USA.*

The Sea World Adventure Parks in the USA are much larger. Sea World Florida covers 81 hectares and is home to some of the largest marine mammals including the famous orca (killer whale) Shamu. Sea World focuses on entertainment, offering rides, shows and attractions that star 800 different creatures including whales, walruses, seals, polar bears, sea lions, otters, dolphins and many others.

▼ A young boy watches dolphins swim by in a well-lit aquarium tank. Places like this are rather like underwater zoos.

Critics of this kind of park say that it is cruel to keep large marine animals captive; they need more space than the park can offer. Sea World says that its animals enjoy what they do, are looked after well by experts and are happy living in the company of others in large tanks. In addition, Sea World is actively involved in education, rescue, rehabilitation and captive breeding work.

case study · case study · case study · case study · case study

Catharine Mason and her Brownie group visited her local Sea Life Centre in Tynemouth, UK for a sleepover.

'It was great, we slept in the hotel next to the centre and were allowed in to the centre at night. They switched all the lights off except in the tanks – it was beautiful. We learned a lot about fish and they even let us stroke the rays.'

6. Hunting and fighting

Why watch animals fight?

Hurting animals for fun is not as common as it once was. As we study and observe animals more, we come to realize how much they can feel pain and distress.

Badgers, although common, are rarely seen, because they are so timid. They live in small social groups in underground tunnels called setts. Badger-baiting, in which dogs were set on captured badgers, often already disabled by blows to the head and legs, was once a popular rural activity in Britain. It was made illegal in 1835 as views on animal welfare changed. Badger-baiting is still practised, however, in great secrecy. London's Metropolitan Police have stated that they fear that it might be on the increase.

▼ *These people are watching a cock fight in a market in Thailand. Many bet on the result of the fight in which one of the birds may die.*

It is difficult to know why people do this. Many spectators bet on the outcome of the fight but, although they are reluctant to talk about it, most just seem to enjoy the bloody spectacle.

Some of the people who take part in badger-baiting would probably enjoy watching a dog fight. This traditional pastime, in which specially bred and trained dogs fight in a ring, has been outlawed in most western countries. Despite the laws forbidding it, there are still many secretly organized fights in Britain, Canada and the USA. The television channel CNN recently reported its growing popularity in Russia.

▲ This pitbull dog is forced to walk on a treadmill in order to build up its stamina and strength for fighting. Dogs are often badly injured, or even killed, while taking part in illegal dog fights.

As with badger-baiting, betting takes place, but the major enjoyment appears to be from watching the two animals engage in a sickening fight, which usually leaves both badly injured and, quite often, one dead. The RSPCA and ASPCA, which campaign to stamp out dog fighting, often have to treat the injured dogs who are abandoned by their 'dog-lover' owners.

The rights and wrongs of fox-hunting

Fox-hunting with horses and dogs is very much a way of life in the British countryside. Songs and paintings celebrate it and for tens of thousands of people 'following the hunt' is part of the traditional New Year festivities.

Recently there has been a heated debate in Britain following the efforts of The Campaign for the Protection of Hunted Animals (CPHA) – comprising the RSPCA, League Against Cruel Sports and International Fund for Animal Welfare – to have fox-hunting outlawed. Opponents say that it is both cruel and barbaric. They argue that at the beginning of the twenty-first century we should not permit a sport in which people gain pleasure from watching an animal being torn to pieces by hounds.

The supporters of fox-hunting say that their opponents do not understand country ways and traditions. They claim that foxes are a pest that often kill hens, pheasants and even lambs. Hunting is, they say, a good way of controlling what is a vicious animal.

▼ *A huntsman leading his fox hounds during a hunt in England in 1999. When a fox is sighted, the hounds will chase it.*

They also argue that the hunts create jobs for people, particularly among those who care for horses. They also help to look after the countryside through maintaining and preserving the areas across which they hunt. Fox-hunters are very critical of what they see as the hypocrisy of their opponents who complain about the killing of a fox, but are not concerned about the damage that a fox can do to farm livestock.

▲ *A fox at bay bares its teeth as the hounds close in for the kill at a hunt in Suffolk, England.*

◀ *These people are hunt saboteurs; they strongly oppose fox-hunting and aim to disrupt the hunt and prevent the hounds from finding a fox to chase.*

Killing animals for their skins

Around 40,000 animals a year are trapped for their fur in the USA. The steel-jaw leg traps most commonly used snap shut on a limb, breaking or dislocating it. The trapped animal usually survives the initial shock and then suffers agony as it tries to free itself. Some animals have even been known to gnaw through their own legs to break free. Many other animals, which are of no value to the trappers, can become caught in the traps and, when found, are just thrown away.

The furs or pelts recovered are sold to the fashion industry to be made into coats, wraps and other fashion garments. A number of animal welfare organizations in the USA are campaigning against this kind of fur trapping. They hope to have the law changed to make it illegal.

▼ *A coyote caught in a leg trap in New Mexico, USA. Traps like this are laid by hunters who catch animals and then sell their skins to the fur trade.*

The annual Canadian seal hunt in which the Canadian government allows the killing of seals has caused a huge international outcry, which goes to the heart of the argument about hunting (see also page 4). Every year the Canadian government issues licences that allow hunters to kill around 250,000 of the 4.8 million seals. The government and the sealers view this as a harvest, rather like a type of fishing.

> 'It takes up to 40 dumb animals to make a fur coat. But only one to wear it.'
> *Slogan on a Greenpeace poster opposing the fur trade*

The organizations that oppose the hunt say that it should be better controlled. They are worried that the hunters are killing too many seals and that the seal population may decline, especially in years of bad weather like 2000 when freak climate conditions killed many seal pups. They are also concerned at the cruelty of the hunt.

The hunters say that people are just being sentimental about 'cuddly' animals that they know little about.

◀ *Fur is still part of the fashion scene, but many designers now think that wearing animal skins is cruel and outdated.*

7. Losing natural habitats

Population growth and extinction

Perhaps the cruellest thing we can do to an animal is to make it extinct. This is something that we humans are, unfortunately, good at. Extinction of a species can happen naturally. Animals like the dinosaurs, for instance, died out due to environmental or climate changes. But humans can cause extinction too. It is widely believed that early humans hunted mammoths and mastodons to extinction.

It is known that Portuguese sailors and the animals that they introduced to Mauritius hunted the flightless Mauritian dodo to extinction in the seventeenth century. In North America the passenger pigeon was hunted to extinction through the nineteenth and early twentieth centuries.

▲ *The dodo, a large flightless bird, was hunted to extinction about 350 years ago.*

▼ *Cutting down forests for timber can destroy animals' natural habitats.*

The growing human population is the greatest threat to the animals with which we share the planet. It is not just the number of humans that is to blame, it is also where we live and how we live. With over half the human race living in cities, we need more space for building. As technology makes more products available to those of us who can afford them, we use more resources to make them.

As we build on open land, mine for minerals, cut down trees for timber and turn more land over to farming, we take living space away from wild animals. These activities destroy the habitats that they need to survive, and so endanger their continued survival in the wild.

▼ *Jersey Zoo's project to save endangered Mauritius kestrels has been a success.*

case study · case study · case study · case study · case study

Modern zoos are concerned with working to protect endangered species. Animals at risk are bred in zoos and, where possible, released into the wild, thus helping to save them from extinction. The Jersey Zoo in the Channel Islands was one of the first to use this approach. In the 1970s there were only four Mauritius kestrels surviving in the wild. Now, with the help of the Durrell Wildlife Conservation Trust, there are more than 800 kestrels flying in the skies above Mauritius. As the zoo's website explains, 'Our symbol is the dodo – a reminder that extinction is forever'.

The threat to sealife

The sea might seem to us to be unchanging and safe. It seems so vast that we cannot harm it. Unfortunately marine animals are amongst the most threatened by habitat loss. Our ports, cities and factories increasingly pollute coastal areas. Pollution is now so widespread that it is found in the flesh of Arctic seals and Antarctic penguins.

▼ *The world under the waves teems with marine life, but even the oceans are being damaged by human activity. Pollution of the sea is now a common problem.*

Some of the most easily damaged animals are whales, particularly those that migrate to breed. Whales are very sensitive to noise and pollution and will soon leave an area if they are disturbed or upset. Pacific gray whales, once common but hunted nearly to extinction, are now only found in the eastern Pacific. They migrate between their feeding grounds off Alaska in the north to birthing nurseries in the lagoons off Mexico's coast.

When a company called ESSA, jointly owned by the Mexican government and the Japanese firm Mitsubishi, revealed plans to open a salt-manufacturing plant at the lagoons used by the whales to give birth, many people were worried. It was felt that the noise of pumps and pollution from the plant could drive the whales away. Ships entering and leaving the planned harbour might hit the whales. As there were no other lagoons that the whales could use, this loss of habitat might drive them to extinction.

At first ESSA refused to change its mind, saying that the threat was being exaggerated. Following a worldwide campaign led by Mexican environmentalists, ESSA finally agreed to cancel the plans in order to protect the whales.

▲ *Tourists reach out to touch an adult gray whale at Laguna Ignacio, the place where ESSA's plans to build a salt factory threatened the last undeveloped calving area for the Pacific gray whale.*

Creating parks for wildlife

One solution to habitat loss that is being adopted around the world is the creation of national parks. In these areas development is tightly controlled or even forbidden in order to protect natural habitats from human activity.

The national parks of the UK, Canada and the USA, although very different in size, have one thing in common: wildlife threatened by agriculture and the spread of towns and cities finds a refuge there.

Ironically, the parks are becoming victims of their own success. As more and more visitors go to the parks to see 'real' nature, they risk damaging the habitats and the animals that live there. There are so many walkers in Britain's Lake District National Park, for example, that they are wearing away the vegetation around footpaths. In some US national parks, bears are changing their feeding habits as they become used to being fed by visitors or stealing from their backpacks.

FACT:
A recent study by the US Nature Conservancy showed that around 33 per cent of US animal species are at risk of extinction.

▶ *A tourist feeds Alpine marmots in Yosemite National Park, California, USA. Parks allow people to be close to wildlife but this is not necessarily a good thing for the animals.*

The largest national park in the world is the Qomolongma Nature Reserve in Tibet. The park, which is the size of Denmark, is unusual in that 75,000 people live and work in it. The people who run it felt that the best way to protect endangered species like the snow and clouded leopards was to find ways for humans and animals to live together. Before the reserve was made, uncontrolled logging was destroying the beautiful valleys and the animals that live in them.

By splitting the reserve into zones, some of which allow a certain amount of development work, the future of the fully protected areas in the middle is guaranteed. The reserve has been so successful that a second larger one, the Four Great Rivers Preserve, is being planned in eastern Tibet.

▲ *Snow leopards are rare wild cats that live in the mountains of Asia. The creation of a huge national park in Tibet has helped to provide a safe home for this endangered species.*

8 . Ready to act

Cruelty or not?

You may have noticed on the labels of some cosmetics or cleaning products the words 'Not tested on animals', 'Cruelty free' or 'Against animal cruelty'. Cruelty-free products (as these items are often called) are becoming much more popular as controversy continues to rage over animal testing.

The people who make cosmetics and cleaning products have to make sure that they are safe for people to use; they could, for instance, cause skin rashes or, worse, serious illnesses, such as cancer, if they were sold in shops without first being tested for safety. For a long time many scientists have believed that the best way to carry out safety tests is to try the products on animals. Lots of tests for different products have been carried out in laboratories that use specially bred animals, such as dogs, cats, rats, monkeys, rabbits and mice for this purpose.

▼ *Animals, such as rats, are used in laboratories to test the safety of many household products before they are put on sale to the general public.*

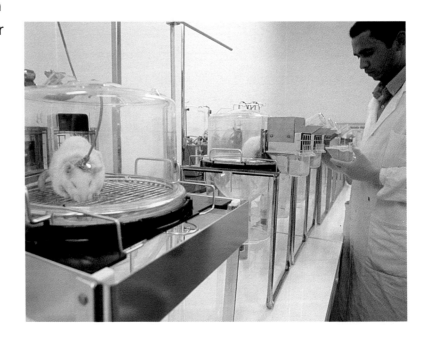

Some of the tests are painful and cause suffering to the animals. They may involve dripping the product onto the animal's eyes or shaven skin, or animals may be force-fed or made to inhale the substance being tested. Many of the tests are for toxicity and cause unpleasant and extreme reactions in the animals.

> 'To my mind the life of the lamb is no less precious than that of a human being. I should be unwilling to take the life of the lamb for the sake of the human body. I hold that the more helpless a creature, the more entitled it is to protection by man from the cruelty of man.'
>
> *Mohandas K. (the Mahatma) Gandhi*

The scientists who do this work point out that they try hard to minimize suffering and that they are acting for the benefit and safety of us all. Many other people, including other scientists, believe that the tests are cruel and unnecessary. Because of the public outcry, many companies no longer use animal testing. The testing of cosmetics on animals is now illegal in the European Union.

Some people are so angry at the way animals are treated by human beings that they campaign in public in support of animal rights. These activists have dressed up in cow costumes to protest at the treatment of cattle infected by BSE or 'Mad Cow Disease'.

Protesters and animal rights

Animal testing is widely used throughout the world for household products, food additives, alcohol and many other things that we use in homes, offices and factories. The largest use, though, is for testing medical products, particularly drugs used in the treatment of illness. In most countries, such as the USA, UK, Canada and Australia, there are laws that control the places where this work is done to ensure that the animals involved do not suffer unduly. The approach of many companies and governments is to reduce testing to a bare minimum.

The opponents of animal testing believe that it should stop entirely, as it is wrong to inflict cruelty on animals just for human benefit. They also say that there are alternatives to using animals, such as computer modelling and the use of synthetic and cloned human skin for testing new products. Feelings run high in the arguments over this issue.

▼ *It is easy for people to forget when they put on their lipstick that the product was probably first tested on an animal.*

Huntingdon Life Sciences (HLS), based in the UK, has been the centre of many protests over animal testing. It is one of the world's largest companies using animals for testing and research purposes. It carries out work for many large companies that produce, among other things, medical products, chemicals for farming and food additives.

The campaigners have tried to close down the company by discouraging investors and customers by generating negative publicity about the company's activities.

Some protesters have sent threats to HLS employees and attacked their property. The company defends itself saying that it does vital work that saves lives and that it cares for its animals. It is also looking into alternatives to live animal testing.

The arguments about the rights and wrongs of animal testing take us back to the questions asked at the beginning of this book. Is it cruel to use animals in this way? That is a something that you must think about carefully and answer for yourself.

▲ *Many supporters of animal testing point out that the trials often help companies to produce life-saving drugs.*

FACT:
In 1999 2,569,295 animals were used in scientific procedures (tests, research and training) in Britain:
63 per cent of the animals used were mice, 0.0023 per cent were dogs.
64 per cent of the procedures were carried out without anaesthetic.
20 per cent of the procedures were for toxicity and 64.9 per cent of the tests were for medical products.
UK Home Office statistics, 1999

GLOSSARY

Ancient Egypt
The civilization based around the River Nile in what is now Egypt, which lasted from around 3000 BC until around 300 AD.

Aquaria
Displays of glass tanks containing fish and other marine and freshwater animals and plants.

Campaigner
A person who tries, through argument, publicity and direct action, to persuade people to change their attitude to something.

Carnivores
Animals and, very occasionally, plants that eat or absorb meat.

Charities
Organizations that help people or animals in need.

Commercial exploitation
Using something to make a profit.

Companion animals
Another term for pets that is growing in popularity because it suggests that pets are not simply the property of their owners.

Domestic, domesticated
Trained or raised to be used to live in homes or in the company of people.

Extinction/extinct
The death of the last member of a species of animal or plant on earth.

Habitat
The natural surroundings and conditions in which animals and plants live.

Hatchery
A place where eggs are hatched out.

Hypocrisy
Pretending to be good or to be concerned about something when you are really as bad as those you criticize.

Humane treatment
Caring or thoughtful behaviour that causes the least possible suffering.

Intensive units
Places or buildings where as many farm animals as possible are kept – the number of animals allowed and conditions in which they are kept are controlled by law.

Ivory trade
The selling of elephant tusks and items made from them.

Mammal
One of a class of fur- or hair-covered animals that suckle their young with milk; includes humans, whales, dogs and cats.

Mature
Adult or grown-up.

Menagerie
A place where captive animals are kept, usually not as big or well-organized as a zoo.

Migrate
To travel long distances, usually in search of warmer weather for feeding or breeding purposes.

Pilot whales
A medium-sized whale that lives in groups that follow a leader or 'pilot'.

Prosecute
To take to court to answer criminal charges.

Refuge
A place of shelter.

Reptiles
A class of animals that includes snakes, crocodiles and tortoises.

Rodents
An order of small gnawing mammals that includes rats, gerbils and mice.

Subsidies
Money given by government to support businesses and industries, particularly when they are having trouble making a profit.

Toxicity
The level of how poisonous something is.

Vet/veterinary
Vet is a shortened form of veterinarian, a person who performs veterinary work, which means the medical care of animals.

Whaling
Hunting whales, usually for their meat, although in the past they were valued for other products such as baleen (bone), blubber (fat) and ambergris (a fat used in perfumes).

Zoo
A short form of zoological garden, which is the term used to describe a place where animals are kept for display.

FURTHER INFORMATION

Animal welfare organizations

These are all mainstream and reputable organizations that promote strongly held beliefs about animal welfare. Their websites and publicity material are responsibly put together and make their points fairly. Occasionally they show pictures of cruelty to animals, which may be disturbing.

The American Humane Association
63 Inverness Drive East
Englewood
CO 80112-5117
USA
Tel: 800-227-4645
Tel: 303-792-9900
Fax: 303-792-5333
Website:
http://www.americanhumane.org

The American Society for the Prevention of Cruelty to Animals
424 East 92nd Street
New York
NY10128
USA
Tel: 212-876-7700
e-mail: education@aspca.org
Website: http://www.ASPCA.org

The Humane Society of the United States
2100 L Street, NW
Washington, DC 20037
USA
Tel: 202-452-1100
Website: http://www.hsus.org

The International Fund for Animal Welfare
Headquarters (USA)
IFAW US

411 Main Street
P.O. Box 193
Yarmouth Port
MA 02675
USA
Tel: 508-744-2000
Fax: 508-744-2009
Website: http://www.ifaw.org

United Kingdom

IFAW UK and IFAW Charitable Trust
87-90 Albert Embankment
London SE1 9UD
Tel: 020-7587-6700
Fax: 020-7587-6720
Websites: http://www.ifaw.org
http://www.ifawct.org (site for teachers and students)

PDSA
Whitechapel Way
Priorslee
Telford
Shropshire TF2 9PQ
Tel: 01952-290999
Fax: 01952-291035
Email: pr@pdsa.org.uk
Website: http://www.pdsa.org.uk

The Royal Society for the Prevention of Cruelty to Animals
Enquiries Service
Wilberforce Way
Southwater
Horsham
West Sussex RH13 7WN
Tel: 0870-010-1181
Website: http://www.rspca.org.uk

Worldwide Fund for Nature – UK
Panda House
Weyside Park
Godalming
Surrey GU7 1XR

Tel: 01483-426444
Fax: 01483-426409
Website: http://www.panda.org

Other useful websites to visit

These websites seek to persuade you that their opinions are right. They use persuasive and, sometimes, emotional language, so read them carefully and make up your own mind on the issues they raise. Only one site, Huntingdon Life Sciences, defends what the other sites call cruelty; it is a good example of a well-put defence of animal research.

Animal Aid
http://www.animalaid.org.uk

Circuses.com
http://www.circuses.com

Compassion in World Farming
http://www.ciwf.co.uk

Dr Hadwen Trust – Humanity in Research
http://www.drhadwentrust.org.uk

FactoryFarming.com
http://www.factoryfarming.com

Huntingdon Life Sciences
http://www.huntingdon.com/index.htm

Links

This site offers links to many other animal welfare pages.
http://www.aspca.org/links

Visit learn.co.uk for more resources

INDEX